Order No. AM 78155
US International Standard Book Number: 0.8256.1273.X
UK International Standard Book Number: 0.7119.2124.5

Exclusive Distributors:
MUSIC SALES CORPORATION
225 Park Avenue South, New York, NY 10003 USA
MUSIC SALES LIMITED
8/9 Frith Street, London W1V 5TZ England
MUSIC SALES PTY. LIMITED
120 Rothschild Street, Rosebery,
Sydney, NSW 2018, Australia

Art Direction: Virginia Rubel
Production: Barry Kaiser
Photo Research: Amanda Rubin

Printed in the United States of America by
Vicks Lithograph and Printing Corporation

Photo Credits: Janette Beckman/Outline Press, Robin Platzer/Images,
Scott Weiner/Retna Ltd., Star File, Scott Downie/Celebrity Photo,
R.J. Capak/London Features Intl., Greg DeGuire/Celebrity File, Vinnie
Zuffante/Star File, Jennifer Rose/Retna Ltd., Barry Talesnick/Retna Ltd.,
Jeffrey Kane/Retna Ltd., John Paschal/Celebrity Photo, Christopher
Helton/Retna Ltd., Steve Granitz/Retna Ltd., Larry Busacca/Retna Ltd.,
Chuck Pulin/Star File

GW00673046

NEW KIDS ON THE BLOCK!
They'll Be Lovin' You Forever!

They've moved into every neighborhood in
every town across the globe—and New Kids
On The Block have made fast, life-long
friends in each and every place!

They are: Donnie Wahlberg, 20, Jon
Knight, 21, Jordan Knight, 19, Danny Wood,
20 and Joe McIntyre, 17. Together, they're
today's newest, hottest singing and dancing
sensation. *Everybody* loves them, *everybody*
wants to know *everything* about them.
It's all here!

NEW KIDS ON THE BLOCK
How They Got The Right Stuff!

New Kids On The Block are so young 'n fresh that it's easy to think they just arrived on the music scene. If ya' didn't know better, you'd think these overnight sensations just got together one day, burst onto the record charts and instantly won the hearts of teens all over the world. You'd think *Hangin' Tough* was their first album; you'd think their SRO whirlwind tour was their maiden go-round the concert scene.

You'd be wrong.

For New Kids On The Block started 'way long ago—Donnie, Jon, Jordan, Danny, and Joe have been singing, dancing and performing together for years! They once had a different name, they once had an album that totally flopped, they were once booed off the stage 'cause no one liked them!!

The 'New Kids story' really *is* one of hangin' tough through uncertain times and disappointing times; of coming through the rough stuff to taste sweet success. It all began in 'Beantown'—that is, Boston, Massachusetts. The year was 1984. It was summer.

New Kids On The Street

Donnie Wahlberg, then 15, was a high school sophomore who was crazy about music and dancing. Living in Boston offered him the opportunity to go to school in a neighborhood other than his own; Donnie was bused to a school in a black neighborhood. There, he grew to love rhythm 'n blues music. He idolized Michael Jackson and taught himself to dance like his idol and do a mean moonwalk. Before long, Donnie earned a rep for being able to move to the groove of his sweet soul music almost as well as the gloved master himself!

Donnie's best friend, *Danny Wood*, was also 15. Danny went to the same school, where he developed a real passion for rap music and breakdancing.

Brothers *Jonathan*, 16, and *Jordan Knight*, 14, were childhood friends of Donnie's and Danny's—they'd all attended the same elementary and middle school. The Knight boys had great singing voices. All their lives they'd sung in their church's choir; Jordan, singled out year after year as a special soloist, was also a natural dancer; breakdancing was his specialty. Jon preferred rap music, at which he became a whiz.

Joe McIntyre was not yet 12 years old that fateful summer of '84—an angelic looking boy soprano with blue eyes and blond hair, Joe

sounded a lot like the young Michael Jackson when he sang. He'd been singing since the age of five and performing in Community Theater. Though well known in his neck of the Boston woods, Joe had never met Donnie, Danny, Jordan, or Jon.

All five Boston 'street' boys had some kind of musical and performing talent. All had ambition, charisma and fresh good looks. None of them, however, would have made it so far so fast if fate—in the form of a man named Maurice Starr—hadn't intervened.

The Mastermind

Maurice Starr was well-known in the music industry. A singer at the start, he cut his musical teeth working behind the scenes with a soul group called The Stylistics. Later, in Boston, he discovered a group of black teens called New Edition. He became their manager and masterminded their early success as a pop-soul band. Maurice also had a hand in the career of Bobby Brown.

In 1984, Maurice and talent agent Mary Alford decided to see if they could find—or put together—a group of white teenagers who could sing, rap and dance to a rhythm 'n blues beat. They were looking to discover—or create—a new musical sensation just like New Edition, but who could cross over, musically, to a broader teen audience.

In other words, they hoped to find a talented troop of teens, train them, and boost them to teen idol status.

Finding The Kids

Maurice and Mary conducted a city wide search for five talented teenaged boys. One of Mary's neighbors was a friend of Donnie Wahlberg's. She'd seen him dance and rap in a local talent show and bugged him to try out for the group.

Danny agreed, but wasn't especially hopeful of this turning into anything. "To me, the audition was just something to do. I was just hanging out." Donnie's dancing dazzled Maurice and Mary for they realized he had something special, he was a natural entertainer. Donnie was NKOTB's first member. Donnie's younger brother Mark, also a performer, had come along on the audition and was signed up right away too, but soon decided this wasn't his thing, so he quit. Donnie was asked if he knew of other talented teens. He did.

"I remembered Jon and Jordan Knight from middle school and what great singers they were," he relates. Jordan agreed to come

for an audition—he brought along his big brother, Jon.

Maurice and Mary fell in love with the Knights. They had beautiful, polished voices and natural performing ability. All those years in church choir had served them well. Jon and Jordan were immediately invited to sign on.

Next, Donnie thought about his good friend, breakdancing Danny Wood and brought him in to audition; Danny became the fourth member of the group.

Still, another boy was needed and once again, it was Donnie Wahlberg who came up with him—and it *wasn't* Joe McIntyre! Instead, Donnie suggested another childhood chum named Jamie Kelly, also a budding singer/dancer/rapper!

Look Ma, We're A Group!

The group was set, except, that is, for one important detail: parents! All the boys were so young, they naturally needed their parents' permission to join. After all, Maurice and Mary had big plans—the boys could not really take a single step toward success without mom and dad's okay.

And in the beginning, their families were wary. Donnie, Jon and Jordan's moms didn't even know they'd gone on the audition—their first inclination was to put the brakes on the whole thing right there and then!

But as each parent met with Maurice and Mary and saw they were completely legitimate, they began to soften. They were assured that being in the group would not interfere with the boys' educations; parents were welcome to come to rehearsals and be part of the excitement, each step of the way. With that, each family gave its blessing to this exciting new venture.

All but one family, that is. Jamie's parents were never comfortable with the idea. Although they allowed Jamie to start with the group, after several months they pulled him out. They simply didn't feel their teenaged son should be exposed to the music business.

A frantic search began for a new, preferably young and cute, member to round out the band: it netted Joe McIntyre. "I tried out on Father's Day, June 15, 1985," remembers Joe, who was only 12 at the time. "Mary picked me up and I was really scared. I went to Maurice's house and tried out. I sang one of the songs the group was about to record and afterwards we got in the car and Mary asked me, 'Well, do you want to be in the group? You've got the part.' And I said, 'Yeah, here I am.'"

The entire process had taken a year.

Training Time

The first order of business was to name the band. Maurice thought of a moniker—and it *wasn't* New Kids On The Block! "Our first name," Donnie reveals, "was Nynuk, pronounced Na-nook. We never did find out what it meant."

Maurice, a prolific songwriter and producer, had music prepared for the boys to learn. He started by having them listen to tunes by the Stylistics and other soul groups like the Temptations. Every day after school, they'd come to a stage at another school and learn the music. Maurice and his brother Soni acted as voice coaches and taught them to sing and harmonize.

But when it came to putting dance routines together, the Boston boys needed no Svengali; they could do that all by themselves! Choreography was their thing and no one—not even Maurice—knew smooth street moves as well as they did. Jordan and Donnie created the steps; Jon, Joe, and Danny picked them up quickly.

Nynuk began to perform at local clubs and festivals around Boston. At least one time, they were *not* greeted with enthusiasm: they were booed offstage! But they kept on.

After a year of rehearsals and club dates, Nynuk was ready to go to New York and land a recording deal. In 1985, the boys auditioned for several record companies and were signed right away to Columbia Records who believed they had, well, the right stuff!

The one problem was their name. No one could pronounce it; it just was *not* happening.

Coming up with a new name wasn't hard. One of the rap tracks they'd recorded kind of said who they were. The song was called New Kids On The Block.

Album Number One: Kid Funk

With high hopes, the boys went into the recording studio and began laying down tracks for their first album. "We did a lot of rap on that LP," offers Jordan, "and a lot of bubblegum type stuff too. It was like kid-funk. That's what we were into at the time."

The *New Kids On The Block* LP was released in 1986 and, led by its first single, "Be My Girl," it went...nowhere! It wasn't being played on radio stations, the record company—in New Kids' opinion—wasn't promoting it; clubs weren't spinning it; MTV wasn't rotating it, not even lightly. The press wasn't impressed; even the teen magazines weren't biting.

Majorly disappointed, still the boys went

on tour to try and spark some interest. They were the opening act for better known groups, but without a record out that audiences had heard, they were met with indifference.

1986 was not their best year, but it wasn't a wasted year either. Looking back, in fact, New Kids found something positive in their early failure. Donnie articulates, "In a way it was a blessing that we didn't have instant success. To have had a hit right away could have been very damaging—probably we would have been walking around thinking we could do anything. But, we took the fall, and realized not everything we do is going to be a hit. We got a little taste of humility." They also got a chance to finish their educations (except Joe) and, "meet girls who liked us for us, not just because we were stars. We weren't." And being able to tell which girls were sincere and which were merely starstruck would come in handy—later on, that is!

Back To The Studio

As a new year rolled around, New Kids On The Block resolved to work even harder. Some changes were already happening. Mary Alford dropped out of the picture and a new manager, Dick Scott, came aboard. Rehearsals became more intense, new music was being learned and the boys were learning to play instruments and to produce some of their music. Donnie, Danny, and Jordan—calling themselves the Crickets—helped out with arranging, engineering and even writing some of the tunes for their second album.

A professional choreographer was employed to sharpen the boys' moves; designers came on board snazzing up their threads with funky hats and mix 'n match jeans. New Kids On The Block had been turned away from success once, but they aimed to come back even stronger. They were hangin' tough.

Breakout Time

It took one full year to record their second album, which was unleashed in March, 1988. A mix of funk and dance tunes like "You Got It (The Right Stuff)" and "Cover Girl," plus swoony ballads like "Please Don't Go Girl," and "I'll Be Lovin' You Forever," *Hangin' Tough*, the LP, nailed down the sound they were searching for.

Still, even *it* didn't take off right away! *Hangin' Tough* floundered until the video for "Please Don't Go Girl" was seen by deejays— then, they started playing it and then, it really rocketed to the top of the charts.

Hangin' Tough has sold over two million copies so far and made New Kids On The Block the first teen group to have four top ten singles from one album! Their singles play constantly on Top 40 radio and shoot to the top of the charts; their videos spin into heavy rotation on MTV; their tours, including their smash double bill with Tiffany, are sell-outs—girls in the audience go wild for them!—the press has discovered them in a big way. And the teen magazines have found permanent new cover boys.

Suddenly, the whole world has caught up with New Kids On The Block and the whole world has fallen head over heels in love with Donnie, Danny, Jon, Jordan, and Joe.

Now, meet 'em one-by-one!

DONNIE
He Loves The Spotlight!

Donnie Wahlberg always wanted to be the center of attention. A natural born ham, Donnie was the kid you couldn't keep your eyes off—since he was one of nine Wahlberg kids, that's saying a lot! Donnie had talent, charm and charisma to the max!

Little Donnie was a happy-go-lucky kid who adapted easily to new situations. Bused out of his neighborhood for school, he made new friends and got into soul music quite naturally. "We all listened to a lot of r 'n b," Donnie says about himself and the rest of NKOTB, "all our school friends were into that."

After school, he'd get together with his friends and form little bands. His first, when he was only 10, was called Risk. "We were terrible," he remembers, "but at the time we thought we were pretty good!" As he got older, he got into rap music and just before NKOTB came along, he and Danny Wood rapped with a group called the Kool Aid Crew. Although Donnie was never the best singer in any of his groups, he was always the one who commanded the spotlight—that's 'cause he'd do anything for attention! "I'd tell jokes, I'd do anything to make sure everyone was looking at *me*," he laughingly recalls.

As much as he coveted center stage, still Donnie had no *real* showbiz aspirations. "I had show-*off* aspirations," he says, "but I was a very realistic thinker. Everyone has dreams about being a star. But I didn't sit there and dream about it all day. I never thought about it because I didn't think the chances were realistic.

Donnie, who's most often the spokesman for the group, will tell you he's the most outgoing and optimistic New Kid. He's the

one to see the silver lining in each cloud—but he's also the one who worries the most—and is the first to defend the band against any criticism. "When people say our music is bubblegum, that insults me," he gripes. "It's like teens don't have the right to make music that's good and appealing to other teens!" He's also the New Kid who's most concerned about their shows. "I can't stand it if I think a show was disorganized," he says, "I really want everything to go well." Onstage, though Donnie doesn't sing lead too often, he makes his presence known. "I'm always out there, waving and winking at the girls in the audience." And don't think NKOTB fans don't know it!

What's Donnie Wahlberg really like? Let *him* tell ya: "I'm wild and crazy—but I'm very caring and lovable!"

DONNIE'S DETAILS

Real name: Donald E. Wahlberg
Birthday: August 17, 1969
Birthplace: Boston, Massachusetts
Parents: Alma and Donald Wahlberg, Sr.
They're divorced.
Brothers: Arthur, Paul, James, and Robert are all older than Donnie; Mark is younger
Sisters: Debbie, Michelle, and Tracey are older
Grew up: In a section of Boston called Dorchester
Height, weight: 5'9", 155 lbs.
Hair & eye color: Blond, hazel
Pets: A dog named sandy and a turtle—named 'Turtle'!
School: Donnie graduated from Copley High School
Instruments: Drums
First ambition: To be a professional athlete

FAVORITES:
Actors: Al Pacino, Jack Nicholson
Actresses: Cher, Jamie Lee Curtis
TV shows: M.A.S.H., Sesame Street and all sports shows
Movies: Rambo, The Outsiders, Dawn Of The Dead
Music: Rhythm 'n blues, rock, pop, rap
Male singers: Michael Jackson, Billy Ocean
Female singers: Janet Jackson, Whitney Houston, Madonna
Groups: Run DMC, One Nation, New Kids On The Block!
Sports: Baseball, basketball, football, swimming, tennis
Sports teams: Boston Celtics, Red Sox, Bruins, Patriots

Food: Kentucky Fried Chicken and
    anything his dad makes!
Drink: Coca Cola
Place: New York City
Clothes: Dramatic looking clothing
Jewelry: Gold rings
Colors: Black and gold

Donnie loves: Being on the road, being in the
    spotlight, being a New Kid On The Block!
Donnie hates: Uncaring, ignorant people
Best habit: "Eating!"
Worst habit: "Laziness"
Spare time: Is usually spent doing sports,
    rehearsing or watching TV
Odd jobs: Working with his dad, who drove a
    delivery truck

What you didn't know about Donnie:
    He's left-handed!
    In high school, he was the only one of his
    friends who didn't make the school
    chorus!
    He's superstitious
    He cries—if his feelings are hurt!

He's the New Kid who:
    Is most outgoing, most energetic, most
    hyper!

JON
A 'Knight' In Shining Armor!

Call him Jonathan. That is, after all, his real
name *and* the one he prefers. It also best
describes his personality, for he's by far the
most serious New Kid, the one who's perhaps
the hardest to get to know, but the one you'll
know best after you win his confidence.

Second to youngest of six kids, Jon grew
up in a household that was always busy and
seriously bustling—that's because his mom, a
social worker, *always* took in foster children.
At any given time there could be close to 20
people living under their one (big!) roof. Jon
learned early on the importance of sharing,
giving and caring. His mom's "open door
policy" taught him the meaning of real
kindness.

Jonathan was a quiet kid who nonetheless
always loved to sing. He was in his school's
chorus and his church choir. But as much as
he loved it, he was never sure if he was good at
it! "I used to sit in front of a mirror and sing,
dreaming about making it big, doubting that I
ever would." And when his brother Jordan
urged him to audition for New Kids,
insecurity almost kept this cutie from going!
"I didn't want to try out," he reveals, "because
I didn't think I could make it. I didn't think I

NEW KIDS ON THE BLOCK

could sing and rap and dance." Luckily, Jordan persuaded him otherwise!

Jon's always described as shy—and he is. Except, that is, when it comes to girls! He's always had girlfriends his whole life—no doubt they're attracted to his sensitive and romantic nature. In his case, still waters run deep indeed!

As much as Jon loves being part of New Kids, he's the one who's still uncomfortable in the spotlight. And when he comes home from a tour, music—and New Kids—is the last thing he wants to talk about. "When I'm with my friends," he relates, "we don't discuss my career. I'm just a normal person, I haven't changed."

We hope you never do, Jon!

JONNY ON THE SPOT!

Real name: Jonathan Rashleigh Knight
Birthday: November 29, 1968
Birthplace: Worcester, Massachusetts
Family data: Mom is Marlene Knight, older brothers are David and Christopher; Jordan's younger. Older sisters are Allison and Sharon. Jon also has many foster brothers and sisters. Jon and Jordan's parents are divorced; the boys don't talk about their dad.
Grew up: In a 17-room, 10-bedroom house in the Dorchester section of Boston.
Height, weight: 5'11", 150 lbs.
Hair & eye color: Brown, hazel
Pets: Siamese cats, birds, fish
School: Jon attended a private high school
First ambition: To be an architect

FAVORITES:
   TV shows: The Cosby Show, thirtysomething
   Movies: Soul Man, Jumpin' Jack Flash
   Memory: Spending childhood summers at the family's cottage
   Music: All kinds except heavy metal!
   Sports: Basketball
   Food: Italian—and *he* cooks!
   Drink: Chocolate milk
   Place: Boston—"it's home!"
   Clothes: Trendy
   Jewelry: Gold chains
   Colors: Black and white

Jon loves: Travel, vacations, dances of the old Motown groups, shopping, being with his buddies
Jon hates: Heavy metal, cheap cologne
Best habit: "Being a good person."
Worst habit: Sleeping too late!

Spare time: Jon likes to work with his
   hands—especially carpentry and
   gardening
Motto: "Work hard. Don't quit, whatever you do."

What you didn't know about Jon:
   He sometimes still suffers from stage
   fright! Before the New Kids first ever
   show, he didn't eat, and his knees were
   shaking on stage!
   He takes vitamins to keep his energy level up
   He says that showbiz may look
   glamorous, but "there's a lot of
   disappointment that people don't know
   about."

He's the New Kid who:
   Is the quietest, most thoughtful, and most
   romantic!

JORDAN
Oh, What A 'Knight'!

Jordan is Jon's younger brother and the two
were always close—but the truth is, they're as
different as, well, 'knight' and day! Where
Jon's shy 'n serious, Jordan's outgoing and
lighthearted. While Jon frankly ducks the
spotlight, Jordan welcomes it with open arms.
Jon's the major worrywart; Jordan's the one
who "always looks on the bright side."

Music has always been the main
motivator in Jordan's life. He could sing
before he could read and he was often a
featured soloist in the church choir. His
dream was to make it big as a singer and
Jordan has always been driven to succeed. As
a teen, he got into breakdancing. A natural
mover, Jordan was soon good enough to teach
other kids how—along with New Kids
Donnie and Danny, Jordan often put on
breakdancing demonstrations.

Being part of New Kids has given his life
meaning, Jordan says, and he's been totally
devoted to the band from day one. Because
he's got a really *great* voice, it's often Jordan
who sings lead on most of the New Kids
songs. The biggest thrill of this life, Jordan
says, was "hearing our song on the radio for
the first time." He quickly admits that
"having that same song flop" was his biggest
disappointment!

Disappointments are certainly fewer now
that New Kids have hit it big and Jordan's
seriously thrilled by that. He loves the fact
that they're successful—but not just for
selfish reasons. He knows that other kids look
up to him now, and he likes that! "I think our
success gives other kids positive role models,"
he says, "because we care about others and
we've very anti-drugs." Well said, Jordan!

JORDAN
Facts, Favorites & Fun!

Real name: Jordan Nathaniel Marcel Knight
Birthday: May 17, 1970
Birthplace: Worcester, Massachusetts
Family data: Is the same as big brother Jon's!
Grew up: In the Knight family home in Dorchester, which is on Boston's south side.
Height, weight: 5'10", 150 lbs.
Hair & eye color: Brown, brown
Pets: Siamese cats, one goldfish
School: Jordan graduated from private school
Instruments: Jordan's getting good on the keyboards!
First ambition: Was always "to sing!"

FAVORITES:
   Actor: Robert DeNiro
   TV show: America's Most Wanted
   Movies: Robocop, The Untouchables
   Music: Rap, rhythm 'n blues
   Male singers: Keith Sweat, Stevie Wonder
   Female singer: Janet Jackson
   Group: Force MD, Beastie Boys, New Edition
   Sports: Basketball, mini-golf
   Food: Chinese food and hot dogs
   Drink: Chocolate milkshake
   Book: Jordan reads all the time—he likes any subject, fiction or non-fiction. He gobbles up magazines, too.
   Place: Boston—"I love the changes of seasons," says he.
   Color: Blue

Jordan loves: Music: singing, playing, writing, listening to and performing it!
Jordan hates: When people stare at him—it makes him uncomfortable
Best habit: "I'm not a worrier."
Worst habit: He's very messy!
Odd jobs: Camp counselor
Spare time: "I like to be alone, listen to music and think things over, get my head straight."

What you didn't know about Jordan:
   He's a leftie!
   He bites his nails (even though he *says* he doesn't worry!)
   He puts ketchup on everything!

He's the New Kid who: Is arguably the most musical of the band, is certainly the easiest to get to know, sometimes parts his hair horizontally on the side of his head and sometimes adds a braid.

JOE
The Blue-Eyed Baby Of The Band
———

Joe McIntyre was destined to be the kid who'd put the New Kids over the top. That was his 'job' from the very beginning! The core of the group was already in place when Maurice Starr went out *looking* for someone much younger than the rest of the guys to complete the line-up, someone sweet and innocent, someone who sounded like a young Michael Jackson or Donny Osmond, someone to be the designated teen idol of the group. Joe McIntyre filled the bill perfectly. He also fulfilled the promise.

It was the song Joe sang lead on, "Please Don't Go Girl" that first hit—and that was because a deejay saw the video with knockout Joe right up front—and knew that once America's teens got an eyeful of *him*, NKOTB was going through the roof!

Yet, it wasn't easy for little Joe personally. He admits that, in the beginning, "I used to wish I was home, just playing football with my friends after school and living a regular life." And as if his tender age didn't make him feel out of place enough in the band, the other guys used to razz him mercilessly! To be sure, it was all in fun, but sometimes, especially when he was homesick out on the road, it used to get to him.

That, however, was *then*. These days, the teasing has stopped and Joe thinks of Donnie, Danny, Jon, and Jordan as "four big brothers," who protect and love him as a real family would.

Of all the guys in the band, Joe's the one who actually came from a showbiz family—a very large family to boot! He's one of *nine* McIntyre kids, all of whom sang, danced and performed in local regional theater. From the time he was only six, Joe was part of the Neighborhood Children's Theater of Boston, a repertory group that put on variety shows all year long. Singing and performing on stage was nothin' new to this New Kid!

The puppy of the group though he is, Joe knows that in certain circles he's the most popular one. He's flattered and appreciative, but refuses to make a big deal out of it. "That would be stupid," he declares.

Success hasn't changed the real life Joe McIntyre in the least. He's held on tight to his old neighborhood friends—among them, he's still best known for his sense of humor. Joe describes himself as "a drummer, funny, loud sometimes, chill and caring."

JOE
A Stack Of Facts!

Real name: Joseph Mulrey McIntyre
Birthday: December 31, 1972
Birthplace: Needham, Massachusetts
Parents: Thomas and Kay McIntyre
Brothers: Tom is Joe's older bro
Sisters: Judith, Alice, Susan, Patricia, Carol,
　　Jean and Kate—all are older than Joe
Grew up: In a section of Boston called
　　Jamaica Plain
Height, weight: 5'6", 115 lbs.
Hair & eye color: Blond, blue
Pets: A Boston terrier
School: Joe attended Catholic Memorial in
　　Boston. He'll soon graduate.
First ambition: "To be a hit at [New York's]
　　Apollo Theater."

FAVORITES:
　　Actor: Tom Hanks
　　Actress: His sister Judy who was on
　　　　afternoon TV in New York
　　TV show: Cheers
　　Movies: Big, Beverly Hills Cop
　　Music: Rhythm 'n blues, pop
　　Male singers: Rick Astley, Michael
　　　　Jackson
　　Female singers: Janet Jackson, Debbie
　　　　Gibson
　　Group: Huey Lewis and the News
　　Sports: Football, basketball, baseball,
　　　　hockey
　　Books: Mysteries
　　Food: Mexican, especially tacos
　　Places: Boston, San Francisco,
　　　　Disneyworld
　　Clothes: Adidas sneakers
　　Color: Navy blue

Joe loves: Hotels, Christmas with his family,
　　and "when everything goes my way."
Joe hates: Dark alleys, war
Best habit: His sense of humor
Worst habit: He makes faces when he thinks
　　no one's looking!
Spare time: If he's alone, he draws; if he's
　　with friends, he'll go to a nearby mall or
　　to an amusement park.
Biggest problem: School! Joe's the only New
　　Kid still in—the only one who must do
　　his homework on the road!
Collects: Baseball caps

What you didn't know about Joe:
　　He's got an incredible memory!
　　Of all the guys in the band, he feels

closest to Danny

He just recently got his braces off!

He's the New Kid who:

Is considered the "little brother" of the group

Gets the most fan mail and the loudest screams at concerts!

DANNY
He's Anything But 'Wood-en'!

Way before he joined New Kids, Danny Wood had a major rep in downtown Beantown as the smoothest mover around—a master breakdancer and rapper. Danny explains, "I always went to school with black kids and I learned from them. It got to the point where black music was my whole life." Not that his parents ever thought so, but breakdancing and rapping eventually became his ticket to success!

Danny's fourth down the line of the six Wood kids—he learned fast how to make himself heard. But when his parents heard that he wanted to make a life in showbiz, they were seriously skeptical. For his part, Danny had no stars in his eyes either. "I thought the chance of being famous was so farfetched," he admits, "I mean, I thought about being an actor on TV, but I'd really only think about it for two seconds, then I'd think about something else. We're all realistic thinkers. We never imagined we could be there."

Credit Danny's realism—and his academic smarts!—for a four year scholarship to the hard-to-get-into Boston University. Even though New Kids came along, he did go to college for a year. Soon he realized, however, "I was learning more with the band than I ever could in school. Even my professors said that I should stick with the group . . . I can always go back to school later in my life."

Eventually, Danny's parents agreed with him—now they're behind him 100%! Like all the other New Kids' parents, they help out with the band's fan mail.

Although Danny's a seriously down-to-earth dude, he has his dreamy, sensitive side too. He collects teddy bears—and he gets scared silly at horror movies! Danny's putting his sensitive side to work in his songwriting—he's just starting and, along with Jordan and Donnie, has written a pair of tunes that'll probably be on the next New Kids LP!

Danny says he's "usually nice, sometimes stubborn, but lovable." Who 'wood-n't' love this tough-on-the-outside, but tender-on-the-inside New Kid?

DANNY DATA

Real name: Daniel William Wood
Birthday: May 14, 1969
Birthplace: Boston, Massachusetts
Parents: Daniel and Elizabeth Wood
Brother: Brett is younger than Danny
Sisters: Beth, Melissa, and Pam are older;
　　Rachel is younger.
Grew up: Dorchester, Boston in an old
　　Victorian house
Height, weight: 5'7", 135 lbs.
Hair & eye color: Dark brown, brown
Pets: Goldfish
Instruments: Danny's getting good on the
　　keyboards
First ambition: "I never had one—until New
　　Kids!"

FAVORITES:
　　Actors: Kevin Costner, Harrison Ford
　　Actresses: Sigourney Weaver, Rae Dawn
　　　　Chong
　　TV show: America's Most Wanted
　　Movies: Star Wars, Trading Places
　　Music: Dance
　　Male singers: Maurice Starr, Jeffrey
　　　　Osbourne
　　Female singer: Whitney Houston
　　Group: Beastie Boys
　　Sports: Soccer, basketball
　　Food: Roast beef, chicken and anything
　　　　his friend Calvin makes!
　　Drink: Water
　　Place: Disneyworld
　　Jewelry: A treble clef and diamond stud
　　　　earring
　　Colors: "All of them!"

Danny loves: Buying clothes, writing songs,
　　recording with NKOTB
Danny hates: Change, being misunderstood
Best habit: Daydreaming
Worst habit: "Being stubborn and not
　　adventurous"
Spare time: Is spent dancing at clubs and
　　"hanging with the homeboys."
Odd jobs: Camp counselor
Motto: "Stick with it, don't give up."

What you didn't know about Danny:
　　He still gets butterflies in his stomach
　　before each show
　　He's working to control his temper
　　He wears glasses

He's the New Kid who:
　　Is the most determined and possibly
　　hardest working
　　Draws a heart after his name on
　　autographs!

NEW KIDS—GIRL TALK!

Girls all over the globe go ga-ga for New Kids—but just what type does it take to turn *their* handsome heads? Well, as ya might expect, each Kid's got his own idea!

Donnie's Dream Date

"Any girl who wins my love," says darlin' Donnie Wahlberg, "well, I can promise her she'll be the happiest girl in the world. That's because when I'm in love, I will do anything for that girl."

Love is something that comes easily for this energetic New Kid—he's the biggest flirt. Donnie's demands are few: "I like girls of all races, shapes and sizes!"

The way to Donnie's heart is to treat him normally. "I don't like being rushed at or grabbed," he explains. His idea of a great date involves dinner, a movie or just sitting outside on a warm night and talking.

Donnie definitely sees himself married some day, but he realizes that day is probably not too near. He's not seeing anyone special right now and although he would go out with a New Kids fan, he's really got little time for romance right now.

Jordan's 'Knights' Are Lonely!

Another New Kid who doesn't have a girl is sweet Jordan Knight. He's been so into his music for so many years that even before New Kids, he really didn't date very much. In spite of his outgoing nature, when it comes to girls, Jordan's a bashful babe! He freely admits, "I've never even been in love!" If you'd like to be the first person to change *that* situation, here's Jordan's advice: "I'm looking for a loving person who likes to have fun and who's not afraid to show her feelings." He cautions, however, that he doesn't think he'll meet his 'one 'n only' when he's on the road touring with New Kids. "I wouldn't want to start a relationship when I'm on the road because I couldn't put any time into it."

Although most of his nights are spent alone, Jordan does know what makes a great date—"going dancing!" That's where he'd take a special girl—when he meets her, that is!

Jon's Somebody's Baby

It's hard to get shy-shy Jonathan Knight to talk much about the kind of girl he goes for. But just watch him, 'cause in *his* case, actions speak much louder than words! In spite of his cool, quiet nature, Jon's been dating since he was very young. There's something quite irresistible about a sweet 'n sensitive guy—girls sense it and react to it immediately! He's never had any trouble with girls!

Is there a special someone in his life right now? You bet! Jon and singing star Tiffany, with whom New Kids have been touring, have been closerthanthis for several months!

Joe—"I'm No Heartbreaker"

He's the youngest 'n most innocent-looking New Kid, but baby blue-eyed Joe McIntyre knows his way around the block when it comes to the opposite sex—that's because, with seven sisters, he's been surrounded by 'em his entire life! Though Joe has no steady at the moment, he's totally clear on what's important. "I go for girls who have a sense of humor—make me laugh and I'm yours," he quips. But there's more to it than that. Joe's attracted to girls with goals, with ideas and interests of their own, who aren't after him simply because he's famous.

Though modest Joe would never admit it, he's the group's sex symbol, the one most fans want on *their* block. "I love girls," Joe responds, "but I'm no heartbreaker." Joe's not a tease; he has every intention of settling down one day. He dreams of a wife and rather large family—"four or five kids," he reveals, "in a big house." The line starts around the block for those who'd like to move in!

Danny's Desire

'Woodja' believe that dynamic Danny Wood isn't *sure* if he's ever been in love?? The smart 'n sensitive New Kid has done his share of dating, but he hasn't gotten real serious with anyone yet.

Danny's description of an ideal girl includes, "long hair, pretty eyes, a nice body, a good personality and a sense of humor." He definitely dislikes girls "who act stupid." He sees no problem with dating a fan, as long as they approach him "nice and quiet!"

Dancin' Danny likes to spend free evenings at clubs where he can really get down and move, so a date with him would probably include the hottest club in town. But Danny's got a quiet side and he'd want to spend some private time, over dinner, getting to know his date too.

Like the other New Kids, Danny sees marriage in the big picture some day... with a family to call his own!

NEW KIDS SECRETS!

On The Road...

They travel with several bodyguards!
It takes three buses to move them, their equipment and backup crew from gig to gig!
They usually sleep on the bus!

Before each show, the boys try to stay loose, then psych each other up by "yelling and stuff!"

In the old days, they'd perform on stage with a tape playing their music in the background; now, they have a real back-up band. Next step: *they'll* play the instruments!

After each show they used to scoot to the nearest McDonalds and discuss how they did. Now, they're too busy signing autographs and meeting new people to do that!

Except for Joe (sometimes) they hardly ever get homesick. "We hang out at home together," the New Kids say, "so being on the road is like seeing someone from home every day!"

Each New Kid comes equipped with a beeper, usually worn on his belt. That's so their moms can contact them any time!!

Joe must travel with a tutor; he's still in school.

To let off steam they'll occasionally have water fights or wrestling matches.

Did You Know That . . .

Two pairs of New Kids have the same initials? (JK, JK, DW & DW)

They consider themselves "normal kids when we get the chance; we like to eat hot dogs and fool around!"

If you put all the New Kids together, add all their brothers and sisters, you get a grand total of 30?!

They were honored in their home town as Gov. Dukakis pronounced April 24 NKOTB day!

New Kids snacks of choice: Doritos with onion dip, double creme Oreos and Reese's peanut butter cups.

No matter what, they'll always be grateful for all the love and support they've gotten from their fans. "New Kids will always be there for you," Jordan says. He speaks for everyone!

The Future File . . .

Includes a Merry, Merry Christmas album and a new studio LP in early 1990.

Includes lots more work fighting drugs. They've performed at various anti-drug rallies and plan to continue to speak out.

Includes learning instruments and contributing more to their new albums, writing *and* producing!

Includes starring in a great big feature film! NKOTB will make their movie debut in 1990, for Disney Studios!

Includes working for as many charitable causes as they can fit into their hectic schedules and always, for peace.